Melodies frc

There's So Much More

Melodies from the Heart and Soul

There's So Much More

A special thank you to Karlee Rose North and Kozakura for helping make this book possible.

Karlee Rose North, editor:

https://linktr.ee/karleerosenorth

Kozakura, cover artist:

https://www.fiverr.com/kozakura

Introduction

There's So Much More

According to *Mental Health America (MHA)*, as of 2022, almost 20% of adults are experiencing a mental illness with nearly 5% of those diagnoses being severe. Additionally, they state that about 8% of Americans in the last year have reported their own substance abuse disorder.

In this book, I discuss my own struggles with mental health issues including bipolar, psychosis, anxiety, panic, trauma, and substance abuse. I am now a student of psychology who is looking to help others understand mental illness better, through connecting with my poems in a raw way.

As you read this book you may find yourself relating to my stories. Please know that this book ends on a positive note and I hope it helps to unleash your own aspirations and individuality for your life.

Trigger warning:
This book covers topics that may be triggering to others such as mental health issues including self-harm, depression, anxiety, substance abuse, and suicidal ideation. Family and relationship troubles and gun violence are also included.

Be sure to take care of yourself while reading.
Enjoy.

There's So Much More

Dedications

There's So Much More

Melodies from the Heart and Soul

Nathan Alan Hamby
I had a thought
but I guess there is a bigger plan
I felt I'd lost
that to my pain, there'd be no end
so I fought on
and somehow ended up alive
I just wish
you were here with your blue eyes

we love you and miss you Nathan

Nadine Blase Psareas
a giving, kind, and pure soul who took me under her wing
when I needed it most
author of bestselling book *Hope Dealers: The Calling, The Struggle, The Breakthroughs, and The Community of Believers*

Mary Maier
my beautiful, loving, and supportive mother

Tim Maier
my father who would do anything for me when I need it most

Sanjay Reddy
for being so incredibly loving, patient, and helping me believe
in myself

to my family and other friends not mentioned who have
taught me things and loved me along the way

There's So Much More

Table of Contents

There's So Much More

Melodies from the Heart and Soul

There's So Much More

Foreword

There's So Much More

Katie Grace is truly poetic with her words, turning her pain into purpose through this work. As a trauma survivor myself, her story empowered me to continue my spiritual path. I've always been drawn to the raw emotion of poetry, philosophy, and how they tie into the human experience as a meat bag on this giant planet floating in the universe--- this book addresses these aspects perfectly.

As a leader in brain health and neuroscience, I can attest that we so often push away our trauma and/or we cope by becoming the victim, the perpetrator, or the rescuer. Katie embraces the natural trauma sequence with grace, self-compassion, and triumph.

As a designer and family life coach, I deeply appreciate her transparency with her family dynamics and how they've impacted her relationships, especially with romance and substances. We need to hear more stories like this to truly grasp improvement as a human, soul, family, and child of God.

With a full and grateful heart,

Fallon Jordan
Certified Brain Health Professional
Designer and Life Coach

There's So Much More

Note to Self

There's So Much More

Melodies from the Heart and Soul

dear Katie Grace,

please wake up with a grateful heart, count your blessings, don't wander far

your thoughts rule your world, they create your reality, what is more powerful?

nothing can be true, unless you surrender to love, even if you don't know what to do

you're not alone, you have support, stay connected and out of your comfort zone

you're still alive, your story carries freedom, for that please strive

we are all interconnected, your life will change the lives of many, don't wish to be dead

for that would keep others, from hearing your story, this world needs mothers

empaths and lovers, of all the world, for we are all sisters and brothers

please stay here and don't give up, someone needs you, you're not out of luck

leave your burdens behind, don't worry about tomorrow, make some friends

I am healthy and happy, a positive affirmation, this isn't meant to be sappy

There's So Much More

it's just the truth, as you and I know, please don't desert us,
and always move

in the direction your heart and soul long for, just for today and
nothing more

so dear Katie, please wake up grateful, have perseverance,
without being hateful

even to yourself, because freedom is in love, and solely on
that you should dwell

think what is true and kind, stay hopeful inside your mind

you are loved and you can do this, you have grace that is so
endless

sing songs from your heart, your unique melody, of
thankfulness in all parts

of your life, you are getting this right, don't deny your fight

your life, even now, is blossoming, something to remind me:

a sunflower that stands tall, pointing toward the sun that will
not fall

still, no matter what your mistakes have been or what
depression tells you, trauma can mend

your story will be used for good, don't give up hope, stay here
as you know you should

Preface

There's So Much More

Melodies from the Heart and Soul

little Katherine Grace
Kulle bug, Katie for short
still growing up
no longer do I hate the first

they said I was small and pure
such a cute kid
sweetness in my veins
cupcake eyes for days

mom said she just wanted
to see me healthy and strong
I loved my imagination, desiring to
know why everybody was hurting

psychology I've always found
so interesting, so profound
the way we can observe
how bias affects us all

constantly learning by observing
whether knowingly or not
just like the world is always turning
nature vs nurture gave me a learning curve

the cards we are dealt
sometimes lock us in a shell
ignorance of ourselves and others
this ignorance is never bliss

may we all rise
as one love, we all have a voice
together; I see now
we are truly better

There's So Much More

The Beginning

There's So Much More

Melodies from the Heart and Soul

my father showed me *Twister*
tumbling around
he always taught me fear
but let me make this clear

he means well
he would do anything for me
just ignorant of someone like me
the highly sensitive person

the introverts, the quiet ones
who are always getting hurt
because words broke me
not sure how, but one day you'll all see

if you don't already know
yet I see it wouldn't be fair
to put blame where
it doesn't quite belong

it's just the way life went
it's just how I dealt with it
see we've all been wrong
and lived false identities

I guess the real crimes
are hatred, pride, and lies
they blindfold us all
they give wicked advice

what's wrong with you?!
what's wrong with me?
I thought to myself
again and again

There's So Much More

one day at home
just down the road
the sirens were, going off
a tornado touched down

I looked around
grabbed what I could
what I cared about the most
and ran downstairs

the safest place
my dad always taught me
back in the closest
was where I stayed

how could mom stay upstairs?
wasn't she scared?
I was, and wrapped in a blanket
as I tried to go to sleep

couldn't quite keep my eyes shut
those sirens were so close
so loud as I wondered
what could happen

every scenario
ran through my brain
just as it would for years
to come of self-shame

this is how I learned
I am not safe
not in this world
not in this place

Melodies from the Heart and Soul

one day came, Jack Ryan
I swear he wouldn't stop crying
my very own brother
a friend, so I'd never be alone

according to my parents
this was the reason
why they had him
we'd always have each other

after mom's dad died
she was thankful for her brothers
them being there with her
all knowing what each other had been through

...who could remember
the last time my parents were even together
affection, grace or love
all of the above

never seen it happen
except for once
one distant memory
the only of positivity

a sweet kiss
as he slammed the door
a common denominator
had already come

more vivid shouts
a time my parents fought
verbal, a bit physical
DVD cases crashing down

There's So Much More

I was on the phone with my friend
at least that's what I thought she was
screaming in her ear
"MOM, DAD"

dropping it, then the running is to come
she heard it all
confronted the next day at school
"I heard it all"

with a smile of death
she giggled and I forgot the rest
but what I remember
was running and running

where could I go?
needed a safe place
to learn and play and grow
where I could stay joyful

wouldn't get that on the streets
where would I go?
yearning to leave
and never look back

betrayed, couldn't see past it
so I went to bed with a heavy head
wouldn't talk
fake asleep

when mom came in
I went dead
she talked to me
not sure what she said

efforts to comfort
the first of many
so much effort I saw wasted
has yet to come

that's when I learned
I am not enough
I am not loved
because I knew

those actions weren't love
it took all my hope
of them being happy
together, forever, a family

There's So Much More

Kat Comes Out to Play

There's So Much More

Melodies from the Heart and Soul

in the kitchen
what a poetic mess
as the rest of the house
my brother and I standing there

I've always loved him
wanted to be the best
big sister for him
as much of his life

hasn't always been quite right
either, as mine has been
shambled with fear
fueling hatred for life itself

the framework of this house
built on broken love, what else?
after awhile our father comes up
up the stairs, you'd hear every footstep

although I remember trying to be kind
all of the time
as my mother said
my father tore him down

this was true
again and again
yet compensation couldn't quite mend
how we both would feel

for years to come
maybe the rest of our lives?
as we fight to not feel
emotions trapped inside

There's So Much More

thoughts wide open
who could heal this way?
standing about 6 feet away
my brother scanned the fridge

I guess he left the door open too long
that's what our father said
which escalated into something
I didn't want to see again

so I stood up, I tried confidence out
for my brother's well being
I thought it could be freeing for us all
boy, was I wrong

my father, you see
he has to be the best
must be right it seemed
no one can out-do him with truth

it didn't take long, just a quick second
before it had gone too far
and now I was the target
as he was in my face

I ran to my room, opposite side of the house
could have been the graveyard
as he followed me
wickedness swallowing us both

my mother wasn't home
he had the house to himself
to parent as he saw best
the ways of his own childhood

Melodies from the Heart and Soul

my father's father
threw him, literally
through a wall, how figuratively
he too was hurt, after all

and it drowned us both
so I screamed out
"I FUCKING HATE YOU"
which had been an accident

hadn't cursed
in front of him yet
that type of language
stayed with my friends

he spanked me in eighth grade
and finally went away
as I texted my mom
"you need a divorce"

please protect us
from this chaos
come home now
we are tumbling down

anger and hurt
pumped through my veins
that feeling would take over
and on myself I'd put blame

what did I do to deserve this?
what is wrong with me?
how will I ever get over this?
how could I make him see?

There's So Much More

I learned then
I am not safe
I learned when
he'd get in my face

so I never stayed home
from a young age
I'd jump from friend to friend
trapped in a cage

I couldn't see I was in deep
my formative years
were swallowing me
darkness seemed to be following me

my own shadows taunting and laughing
they were hoping I'd screw it all up
I had no clue what would follow
this was the birth of Kat

Kat was angry at herself
pain, blame, and shame
engulfed my life
for years to come

so at fourteen years old
I hit my first bowl
marijuana, on April 20th
420, who wouldn't want to try it?

no I didn't get high
but the feeling of rebellion
the smell, the adrenaline
I was in love

then came my first beer
warm, hidden in the ceiling tiles
another way to rebel
and dance with the rush

I didn't really get drunk
but I was stuck
on trying things and lying
about what I was doing

Kat was secretive
and made more friends
the edgy ones
who knew all about the buzz

the first time I got stoned
my fears hit me hard
so I absolutely hated it
and begged God to take it away

I promised I'd never do it again
the first of a million lies
defined by buds
as I tried it again and again

often to have the same event
psychotic features so fearful
every time I swore to myself
I'd never smoke it again

after many summer experiments
I started high school
where depression took over
every cell in my body

There's So Much More

anxious at every hallway turn
every classroom
myself, and almost anyone else
I truly hated deep to the core

my relationship with my dad
got worse and worse
anger pumped through my veins
taking over at the sound of hatred in his voice

angry and threatening
to my mother or brother
if he truly loved me
wouldn't he love the people I cared about most?

I constantly wondered
and couldn't understand why
time after time
not realizing it wasn't my fault

Kat would come out to play
more frequently
Katie was a cheerleader
Kat made friends with the seniors

they knew how to party
now I had gotten drunk
I tasted the sweet numbness
and didn't think I could get hooked

constantly looking over my shoulder
anxiety provoked
a deeper depression
I bottled it all inside

Melodies from the Heart and Soul

who could I talk to?
I'd been a burden
I was convinced
I was truly alone

my greatest desire
a love to light my heart on fire
but time after time experience proved
to Katie that this would never happen

I was broken in so many ways
questioning the existence of God
how could he be real?
all knowing, and let me feel this way?

the cards I had been dealt
didn't seem fair
embarrassment
constant fear

dad talked about fearful things
all the twists and turns
I didn't want to listen to more
I wanted to walk out the door

I got good at tuning him out
and constantly went out
saving his lunch money, starving weekly
with a bag of chips just to buy drugs

when the weekend comes
I'll be alright
I can smoke and get drunk
Kat overtook Katie

There's So Much More

the buzz was my best friend
but the buzz become swallowing
I had no moderation
I was ready to get fucked up

my senior friends
invited me over before cheer practice
I could get high
on a Friday night

glad to see them
excited for once
because I knew
what was to come

that was the biggest bong
I had seen thus far
scientific bubblers
they said it was three-hundred dollars

I remember that summer
Kat hit one before
it was broken and taped together
I had to hit it hard, to get any smoke at all

so I thought when they asked
if I had hit one before
I knew what I was doing
so I simply said yes

that was enough for them
as they passed it my way
their jaws dropped from their face
I had cleared a full pollen bowl

Melodies from the Heart and Soul

why were they surprised?
smoke filled my eyes
coughing like never before
I didn't even know

what kief was at the time
hadn't smoked in a couple of weeks
tolerance was low
but high I could get

and that's exactly what I got
they tried to pass it again
but I said I was good
one last thing I remembered

was walking towards the truck
I had passed out in the back seat
as we drove away
before even making it out of the neighborhood

I was in a very realistic dream
in a pinball machine
only to wake up
and realize the ball was the car

I saw I was in the back
yet I was convinced
I was driving around
through town, hurting people

so much happened so fast
only in my head
the worst of nightmares
a truly living hell

There's So Much More

it was grand theft auto
driving over people
hitting cars and buildings
police chasing

helicopters following
I was on the news
like other mad men and women I'd seen
a murderer, yet I had no intentions to harm

my friend, scared now himself
he took a recording of me screaming
"I'M NOT TOUCHING ANYONE"
"I'M NOT TOUCHING ANYONE"

after he kept telling me I was okay
I still didn't believe him
I couldn't come down
I felt I was meant to be put 6 feet in the ground

he dropped me back off at school
jacked up, I puked in the bathroom
greened out, anxiety ridden
the first of many pictures

of Kat passed out on a floor
I didn't make it to cheer practice that night
funny enough, my mother was to pick me up
with her friend, and take me to the tattoo shop

hours later
I barely pulled myself together
to get my navel pierced
I was so under the weather

Melodies from the Heart and Soul

how did she not truly know
the extent of what was up?
I didn't talk
nodding in and out

in the back of her van
even when
the piercer was talking to me
I certainly felt no physical pain

this was not the first
or last time
I made a fool of my mother
someone who had shown so much love

you'd think after that
and more hallucinations sober
I would have stopped
never to touch it again

like the caterpillar on the ceiling
the faces popping out of the wall
Katie wanted answers
Kat overtook

I wanted to escape still
and that was the only way I could
everything seemed to get worse
and worse, and I got more drunk

I then found a new best friend
not sure of the first time I met her
xanax made Kat come alive, a magic pill
I'd think everything could get better

There's So Much More

soon I'd be sniffing them at school
and hating myself even more
the first time I self-harmed
I was drunk for over twenty-four hours straight

probably fifteen
at my best friend's house
where there were so many people
we'd gather around, yet I felt so alone

so alone I went off
and attacked my leg
as much as possible
where no one could see

I pushed people away
rejecting them before they could
reject me, a strong fear of mine
my grade school friends

I didn't stick with
no matter how long I knew them
I gravitated towards the party crowd
you already know why, they knew the buzz well

my parents never questioned
why I hung out with older people
my father had a hunch
and I was breaking my mom's trust

my mother believed my lies
but my dad saw me hungover
he was always the one
to pick me up the day after

Melodies from the Heart and Soul

more pictures stocked up
on my friends' phones
of Kat passed out on the floor
after puking, next to the toilet

still seeking, still searching
for true love
sex, I'd hope would be the way
to find what my soul thirsted for

yet it tore me down more
because they never stuck around
used me and disposed of me
threw my heart on the ground

I withdrew from school
a big argument with my parents
they were all in until the night before
I had fell through a ceiling, oops

I had been so drunk
off Bud Light Platinums
running across boards
of an unfinished floor

just to smoke a cigarette
my leg did catch me
so I didn't fall 26 feet down
but up to my thigh, I made a big hole

my dad had to fix the next day
I hated school, myself, and everyone else
so deeply at this point
leaving was the only way out

There's So Much More

I became a bigger pot head
xanax was my closest friend
cigarettes kept me going
and I had my first taste of cocaine

the rush was like nothing else
but I couldn't get my hands
on much at the time
still thinking I had no big issues

comparison is a vicious trap
and these friends I made
were the absolute worst for me
self-centered and so controlling

I got sick of it all
I felt deep in my heart
a pull to stop
and that I did

I isolated myself
and I didn't have the chance
to keep screwing up
I was sober for a few months

but my mother was my only friend
and I had no authentic connections
I wasn't honest with anyone
and still longed to feel loved

I still hated myself
I still felt so alone
until the day I met J
he was my age, same grade

Melodies from the Heart and Soul

he gave me attention
I had hope
although I knew he wasn't good for me
J was battling huge shadows of his own

I attracted the bad guys
I made excuses
Kat loved it
Katie shrunk back in fear

I was so tired of it all
having no friends
I needed real love
I needed to learn to cope

with what I grew up with
what I experienced at school
how I felt inside
all the tears bottled up that I never cried

J was terribly sick
xanax binges for days
that I grew so unattracted to
yet I thought I could mend him

one day I was so pissed off
he was on another binge
turned into another person
not the person I loved

I showed up at his place
just to tell him xanax or me
like that would really work
didn't know what I walked into

There's So Much More

the funny thing about bars
they made you feel invincible
as all anxiety and common sense
completely leaves you

so him and his buddies
thought it was a good idea
to short some drug dealers
on an ounce of pot

I was high on pot myself
still not really in the right mind
although I didn't plan it with them
fire was coming to our sides

J said of course he'd choose me, a lie
I learned people must stop for themselves
so they robbed these guys
who ended up having guns

oh boy, this was not fun
a guy got away on foot
chasing through the woods
they persuaded me to pick him up

a gun in my face
and white shoes covered
in his buddy's blood
J wasn't even phased

an ambulance and ten cop cars
pulled up into the dark brook
police took us down to the station
my old Buick taken as evidence

Melodies from the Heart and Soul

they wanted to charge me
with accomplice to robbery
thankfully they decided
what the real crime was

pulling a gun out
and threatening to shoot
yet I still stayed with him
caught in lust and fake love

I wasn't myself
pushed my friends away
one day I looked in the mirror
my eyes blood shot and glazed

to my surprise
I saw a stranger
looking back at me
as I knew this was simply not who

I was meant to be, not living in my potential
yet I stayed with him
until the summer after I graduated
when he cheated on me

that was it, I was fed up
so I went to his house
5am, tore our pictures to shreds
left them on his bed

so he could see what he had done
I cried like never before
I had to run the other way
I ran as fast as I could

There's So Much More

I couldn't see hope
because I had none
I was torn up, inside and out
and I wrote down these words:

baby you're toxic, you were bad for me
no sense trying to live out a broken dream
took off the chains, to feel the pain
but rain always leaves us a brighter day

as I tried to find that hope
I could never find
inside of myself
I dug deeper into my own hole

Recovery or am I Still Running

There's So Much More

Melodies from the Heart and Soul

Katie and Kat
they fought often
Katie still in there
she talked to herself:

dark fades to good
like dusk turns to dawn
no looking back
my old life is gone

but what happens
when the voice starts coming near
dark and seductive pulling the past here
she screams that she wants something more

she feels so alone and bored
oh honey please just one more time
she begs and persuades
it's so hard to say no

the voice of wisdom fights back hard
with anger they battle and brawl
wisdom gets stronger and darkness falls
but then the days come where

the wise loses its wisdom to fury
in a hurry it throws its hands up in the air
fuck it, I'll do it, I'll fall down
fuck it whatever I'm tumbling now

all that was worked for lit up in a second
fury was not the key
I need compassion to rescue me
I understand you're not where you want to be

There's So Much More

just listen here, you haven't gotten the chance
to get to where you're going, you're only in transition
building yourself and learning who you are
There's So Much More than this

there are people out there just like you
you can get better
you can get stronger
honey, it won't be too long now

as the old fades away
to nothing more
than poetry and a distant memory
a testimony to all

but Katie and Kat felt alone
she sensed fake people
even in church
perfectionism strikes deep

a facade
a false face
a front
even in front of God?

Kat was angry
Katie, still hurting
striving and trying
overly grinding

Katie wanted peace
knew happiness as a glimpse
known to be a way of travel
not a destination

but still, so hard to lay down
lay down every burden and fear
at the foot of something
Katie was taught to fear herself

There's So Much More

Mrs. to Be

There's So Much More

Melodies from the Heart and Soul

sweet baby C
heard so much good of his name
such a cutie
and a heart made of gold

so responsible
I thought
always active
moving forward

traded a good job
for a pretty good job
an even better one
just around the corner

that's where I met him
Mansell and Hwy 9
lovely coffee shop
and with him I felt on top

could this really be something?
or is it just another thing?
another guy to tear apart my heart?
what will this be actually?

after a long year
manic depression's laughter
gripped Katie tighter
angry when there was no beer

no clearance for self-love
truly deceived by the images
of doves and love
the striving continued

There's So Much More

until he pushed her away
enough for Katie to leave
suffocating trauma
we all have to eventually face

I packed all my stuff
as my father unpacked his truck
he picked me up that day
and took me home to stay

Rx: C17H21NO4

There's So Much More

so here I was again
after I thought I had it all
my whole life
had been planned out

I guess life had for me
a different route
as I found myself
on my parent's couch

sleeping there every night
deep depression
where was the light?
because I felt no hope

back in this toxic place
where it all began
where I had to face myself
and all my fears

I couldn't handle the pain
and from my dreams
I had grown so far away
quite honestly

I don't know if I tried
or if I just ran to hide
as I've always done
efforts to protect myself, strung out

drown myself in mom's beer
more frequently drinking
a higher quantity nightly
was the best Kat could feel

Melodies from the Heart and Soul

my brother, I learned
had smoked my pot at age ten
stolen from me when I was fifteen
I had no idea

so he did what I did
at a young age
and smoked THC everyday
but there was a new thing

in this day and age,
concentrates, dabs, wax
THC to the extreme
was what I was constantly around

he always had it
never stayed dry
in a pen or a rig
it intrigued me, as it always had

never was good at saying no
so I asked for a hit
Kat was crossfaded
Katie; nowhere to be found

alcohol and THC seemed to mix okay
I wasn't in such a panic
as I was at a younger age
always had been curious though

as to why I kept coming back
to weed, still didn't see
I was tangled
and mangled, couldn't breathe

There's So Much More

this became a daily thing
I got my own dab pen
it lasted a whole month
you see, reverse tolerance happens

it had been a couple years
since I had that particular dance
that love-hate relationship
sparked in me yet again

self-hatred had always been there
the ill drugs were still
the only way I knew
how to live and thrive

to truly feel alive
something was always missing
seeking, seeking, seeking
obsessing over bad things

no matter what my counselor said
or the psychiatrist
or my consciousness
not to smoke pot or do drugs

Kat was so excited
that she was coming back strong
regrets pulled at my mind
my heart was broken

so I got connected
with Pat, an old friend
the one who I first
had done cocaine with

Melodies from the Heart and Soul

we smoked and drank
sex on fire
could he fill my hearts desires?
funny thing is

I guess all my x's do live in Texas
but I had moved out, moved on
as baby C didn't reach out
or ask me to come back

he must not want to make things right
he was probably glad I was gone
a burden, a love gone wrong, I thought
I was completely convinced

I'd never hear from him again
until the day my car was parked
at the complex all night
his best friend saw, confronting dice

Kat and Pat played games with him hard
Kat had taken over completely
no remorse, not for these things
the numbing had only begun

Pat mentioned an old friend
who I'd meet up with
the very next week
a bar that became my favorite

I was always wasted
stoned out of my mind
floating through the bar
comfortably in a daze, shoes off

There's So Much More

couldn't drive home
a dear old white powdered friend
I said no at first
a bump in front of me

was all it took
I changed my mind quickly
and that was it
pure taste I felt

numbness I'd certainly get
physically and mentally
I indulged in the drip
of course, this escalated quick

another old friend came around
much older than I was
musical and attractive
I had a huge crush on him

he didn't drink
didn't care if I did
he didn't smoke
didn't care that I did

his friend was blow
and that excited me more
staying up all night with him
diving into more and more

I was so supportive of his art
his music, his videos
anything he'd show me
I was interested in truly

Melodies from the Heart and Soul

but did he care for me?
again I thought I had lost
the belief that I am not enough
my mind constantly reinforced

a theme in my life
yet I felt I was too much
at the same time
couldn't quite get things right

worthless, garbage
wishing for death
to drive my new car
recklessly off a cliff

I truly wanted death
again, again, again
self-harm was still Kat's friend
self-hatred to the core

behaviors I didn't know
how to unlearn
still functioning at work
most of the time

but there were the days at work
in the psychiatric clinic
I self-harmed in the closet
needing to take that mental health day

promised to me
yet my boss never said I could
I needed to push through
and keep working hard

There's So Much More

pull myself together
fake another smile
white knuckle it through
just like others taught me to do

working on my addictions counseling course
I was living a double life
filled with deceit and self-loathing knives
for myself, and everyone else

the dab pens evaporated into my lungs
I now could go through a whole cart
in twenty-four hours
and I've got a second job

vape shop, just down the road
and finally out of Katie's parents' house
what a toxic household
Kat truly hated being there

where the pain began
traumatized by ideals completely
the vape store was great
at least for a while

the people smoked at the store
perhaps didn't know for sure
I would do coke in the bathroom
geeked up just to work

constantly high, the only way
to pull myself out of depression
I couldn't function
without substances revv'n my engine

Melodies from the Heart and Soul

I felt like dying everyday
just wanted to close my eyes
at night, and feel alright sometimes
my life became a mess

my bedroom torn up
dirty laundry piled up
my car was even worse
lined with trash

self-hygiene declined
falling down
tumbling now
everything was a wreck

a metaphor
for how I felt inside
I wasn't taking care of myself
I couldn't pay my own bills

I had no will to live
I couldn't go on this way
I wrote a poem
to express how I felt:

I think I'm going crazy, living a double life
I thought it couldn't break me, but now I'm thinking twice
my brain is really hazy, and I just want to get high
this is finally phasing me, with self-hatred at my side

wanna die?
how can I break out of here?
how can I make this clear that I don'l like where I'm going?
how can I get where I want as I'm not showing the best
version of us?

There's So Much More

at my second addictions counseling class
I met a man my age
he worked for a sober living
we became friends online

I reached out to him, told him I was struggling
he asked about my history
as they all thought I was in recovery
he said if I ever needed a place to stay

to speak to him
yet I wasn't honest
how could I be?
I was full of shame

finally, I was so fed up
I told him so
I was full force into the drugs
going downhill rapidly

my chaos tangling me
I needed help
perhaps the first time I had been honest
and he helped me out

but I needed my parent's support
the hardest thing of all
was to confess to them
where I was at

what I had done
my life was in shambles
I couldn't go on
living the way I was

so I bit the bullet
and let them know the truth
they were angry
said they wouldn't help me

that I couldn't take care of myself
that I needed to move back in
like they could help me?
like we could be a family?

I told them I'd rather be dead
I told them I'd figure it out on my own then
they researched and thought
until they supported my decision

There's So Much More

Seeking Help

There's So Much More

Melodies from the Heart and Soul

I'm tired of being sick
and I'm sick of being tired
don't want to fake a smile tonight
don't want to be a liar

no one really cares
like they say they do
because who would dare
walk with me in my shoes

these burdens I've been facing
I try to cast them on God
all it's done is gotten me angry
can't seem to follow his rod

sometimes my brain is in a fog
as I obsess over my thoughts
I do not have a bird's eye view
being controlling won't make me new

yet my God is full of love
he would never leave me in the dust
he sees all and protects me
from myself, I am asking for eyes to see

the serenity prayer I pray
with faith and hope that one day
my heart's desires and dreams fulfilled
his plan is much greater and so skilled

so I'll walk in gratitude and love
and stay connected to the spirit above
this is how I'll win the battlefield of the mind
by confronting my subconscious lies every time

There's So Much More

they pop up
like an evil whack-a-mole game
don't want to give up
don't want to chase fame

I need to do this for myself
humbly coming around
not to seek validation
in anyone or anything else

but still, cunning lies
capturing evil images in my mind
bipolar; a mixed state
such a disorder, needing clear order

I'm so depressed
I don't know what to do
in the interim time
trying to make my life new

depression is gripping
isolation and silence
I need an awakening
I can't go on like this

I am so low
I don't think I could take another blow
trying to remain calm
I wrote down these words:

I am either in heaven or I am in hell
a sea of bliss or not so well
I try to find peace but I dwell
can someone help take me out of this shell?

Melodies from the Heart and Soul

maybe this is the reason I have not found peace
I am just wishing someone could see
my face and spirit, inside to the real me
because I love all people, but they seem to always leave

maybe this is a lie but it is why I am so scared
my demons laugh at me from deep inside their layer
the deck of cards I have been dealt just does not seem fair
but my God has said to me that he truly cares

There's So Much More

A Miracle

There's So Much More

Melodies from the Heart and Soul

truly I heard, now truly I see
life lessons are always dancing with me
and now, how simply profound
the way this addict may now

truly believe, Love Out Values Everything
I say thank you to all
woman or man
those allowing love

guide me by the hand
the heart of mankind
can truly be deceitful, the battle of our mind
thoughts are so powerful

simple neuroscience sees these pathways engraving
longer and stronger, reinforced daily
I'm so grateful, just for today
I'm so thankful, perhaps the rest of my days

may be filled with intuitive wisdom
clearance to love myself as well
oh what a contrast!
I felt as an angel, fallen, in hell

truly at rock bottom
again, yet again
then hyped to the max
obsessions, divert, outplaced

my head is really spinning around
because out of place I put myself
before age 7, I knew to torture
even torture myself

There's So Much More

making heaven or earth
my own living hell
now that I know what I know
I truly see the peace

now that I know what I know
purity is freedom, without my reigns
now that I know what I know
faith can love myself, too

now if you know, you know
why the law, the prophets
hang, on to an imaginable love
as gentle as a dove

true love washes our thinking
for even murder starts in the heart
the power of life and death
are in the tongue

entertaining negative thoughts, hatred for
what life already gave us
led to the fall, of all humanity
we are all human, will you join me

in asking for eyes to see truth
even through my own cobwebs
my God, justly in love, pulled through
I asked for my own miracle

Katie was just a little girl
hiding, lying, and overly grinding
would try to define me for,
two decades to come, undone

Melodies from the Heart and Soul

I kept fighting and hiding myself
an obsessive addict perhaps
schizophrenic tendencies
a manic depression head spinning

again and again, but God
he washes me with mercy
and took my mind in love
an awakening needing

truth and peace
my equations have been solved
I feel freedom to be me
strength to stand up for my new boundaries

I don't care if anyone laughs at me
because I've been in their shoes
perhaps a little different but,
still, all the same roots and rules

this tree of life can't be computed
only by the Alpha and Omega
the King has allowed me to sing
my praises and allows me to raise

you up too, not by fixing, just by being
you see, I even lost control of my own mind
love captured my mind
purely by grace, I am found

~ just breathe ~

There's So Much More

miracles surrounding me
loving power defines me
rhymes wash through me
in a whole new light

my own darkness, turned
to enlightenment, a miracle even
through bipolar I
rejected by the world

I am rejected no longer
I have gifts and wisdom
truly marked as
a wounded healer

Goodbye for Now, I Hope to See You Soon

There's So Much More

Melodies from the Heart and Soul

another goodbye
another time
I must leave you on your own
you used to feel like home

but now we are so far apart
you're two different people
wrapped into one, just as I was
how am I supposed to figure it out?

which face will stay?
that I can't say
only my God knows the truth
who you really want to be

vs. what pulls you down
you're giving in
again my friend
slowly slipping down and out

a taste I gave
of your true heart
a life for true love
out of the cunning dark

but dark you've known
and dark you'll stay
till you decide to fight this match
war did strike on the edge of your life

bloody battles of strife
so much you'll lose that you've always known
yet **There's So Much More** you'll gain
as we lift each other up

There's So Much More

over that mountain you built yourself
as treacherous as it may seem
in my dreams I see you happy
with all your spirit deserves

you are healthy as your relationships
and living truly for love
I dream to see you one day in heaven
the only place the madness ends

ultimately at peace
a rest you don't get from sleep
brothers and sisters we can truly be
I want to set you free

from what you think is holding you down
but jokes on me
if I think I can figure it all out
you're in control of one thing my dear

and that is your own decisions
sending good vibes
that you'll fight the good fight
and not give in to hatred, the pure evil

all I can do is hope and pray
that one day you'll be okay
free from anguish and pride
we have all been living in

to see again the light
darkness has blinded all your life
your family, friends and more
but there is hope and grace

Melodies from the Heart and Soul

to pull you out of that place
God can take your disaster
turn it good for so much more
than you can imagine right now

rather than spinning around
this haunted merry go round
carousel of wicked licks
its parts look friendly

some even of heavenly pleasure
but once you hop on
one day you'll find
it's a life sucking constant circle

the same places
all the same frequencies
just twisted a little different
all of it coming from

that scheming operator
wickedly smirking behind the buttons
laughing that your stuck in his trap
that never ending fair

he'll tell you it's free to play
so you can save your coins for yourself
there you went now here you are
on that constant cycle

crashing down on that worn out merry go round
where you'll hear no true laughter
you won't find true joy, love, or peace
only self-seeking shadows

There's So Much More

torment you they will
until you feel more hopeless than before
and the ride doesn't stop
to let anyone off

and behind his control panel he will stay
as he sends out his friends to mess with you
according to his evil plan
even still, you have a decision to make

to end the ride in one of two ways
that rope you see
seems so easily in reach
used to end it all, take the easy way out

or so it may seem
that is what the carousel engineer hopes for you to do
kill all hope, torment those that knew you
your only other option is to jump

it's spinning so fast
the jump seems quite impossible
but at least you know now
you want to have that life before the fair

you can barely see the light
but you know it's still there
bracing yourself
looking at what is all around you

you finally make the jump
knowing it's what you have to do, last straw
this is it, hurting like never before
perhaps repairing yourself seems worse

facing yourself and all the shadows
it gets pretty scary, almost terrifying
but freedom is the reason
what you're really searching for

how will you put back all the pieces?
you constantly wonder
all you can do is trust the process
put one foot in front of the other

with arms stretched out wide
God promised never to leave you
love's energy is here
no matter where you've gone to hide

Love
Out
Values
Everything

There's So Much More

Poetry of Memory

There's So Much More

False Evidence Appearing Real

lacking the discipline
the drive, the motivation
or am I just being defined
by the lies in my own mind?

they tear me apart
they break my own heart
living out of fear
how could my vision be clear?

There's So Much More

Trauma

in and out of time
another wrong on my mind
imperfections try to define
me, myself, and I

anxiety stirring
while paranoia pokes through
why are they looking at me?
what am I gonna do?

mood dips low
after getting too high
no one knows
about the tears I don't cry

my mind is never boring
with all these racing thoughts
yet somehow, I still feel lonely
out of place, but what's the cause?

little Katie Grace, I think about you often
looking back, on the past
it kinda makes me sad
in fact, I think I almost lost it

exhausted, doing all of it
my coffin, it still don't fit
feeling lost but I won't quit
feeling lost but I won't quit

you always hoped
one day your fear would be dissolved
has that gone away?
hate shouldn't have been involved

look at what it did to me
desiring love infinitely
suicidal, scared to leave
at times, my life's a mystery

Melodies from the Heart and Soul

but I know one thing
can't keep trying to figure it out
in silence my ears ring
brain buzzing on all the how's

what ifs and doubts
so I play my music loud
drown away another sorrow
guess I'll see you guys tomorrow

There's So Much More

Suppressed

sweetest complexion
beautiful affection
mask over concrete walls
won't let you see me fall
not sure if I'm falling now
how I wish my feet were firmly on the ground
I've suppressed trauma and emotion for so long
still, I don't think I'm too far gone

Story

there was a little girl
who struggled to find an outlet
often in a daze, a day dream
escaping what made her feel down and

she took a pencil to her folder
made some beautiful art
in class a girl not much older
tore the thing apart

the older girl must not have known
things weren't great at home
for on my face it was never shown
and I felt truly alone

push it away
there's always
another day
to play

never taught to process
at least healthily
never taught boundaries
respect for others, especially

an unbound and unwound child
would run wild
while I also ran from sadness
and other feelings I deemed bad

perfectionist at a very young age
too scared to get in trouble
never stopping to say, "wait"
reinforcing my own bubble

of illusion
delusions
and confusion
but she was only a child

There's So Much More

she was only a hurt child
and as she grew, she hardened
still her heart shines like gold
under layers of a toxic wasteland

popular now
yet still felt out of place
a cheerleading flyer
looking to move at another's pace

comparison and
keeping up a face
a facade all along
why would they think the real me is great?

so she became a hurricane
and loved to rebel in secret
said some mean things along the way
that even cut my own self deeply

regret piled up
escaping again and again
how could I get up?
I've mistaken all my friends

this is why hurt people hurt people
this is why mental health is important
this is an apology for all the wrongs I did
this is hope that you too can forgive yourself my friend

Rejecting

depression is coming so strongly over me
I feel alone and unloved
rejecting myself
but I don't know why
besides it's just the life I've lived

I wish I could hide away
but I don't want to go
I just want relief

motivation stripped away
sadness overtakes
another day
here and gone away

Walk Down to the River

your beautiful yet long face cries
although no tears are in your eyes
a little walk down to the river
may make it all a bit better

you're living life in disguise
learning yourself through your own rhymes
a little walk down to the river
may make it all a bit better

energy clogged and condensed
I'm not sitting on the fence, just inclined
to walk down by the river
let nature allow me to breathe better

out of the endless blue sky
clouds puffed up high
the river sings to me
as trees dance to the breeze
designed are rocky cliffs
where I sit to make a wish
to grow, be whole
it is better to know

my soul is warmed
must I mourn?
a little walk down to the river
may make it all a bit better

Blue Sky Sunny Eyes

blue sky
sunny eyes
that's what I call
myself

I can't deny
or try to hide
the fact that I fall
and dwell

on my mistakes
as the waves crash in
demonic laughter
surrounding

this can't be my fate
as I have passions
I'm chasing after
drowning

I must look up and around
not trip on what's behind
I've fallen on the ground
but still this time

I can stand up
seven times seven
forgive this bump
and learn a lesson

a powerful testimony
is what I hold
so I will stand bold
my story will be told

There's So Much More

to help others through
the chaos and tears
if only we always knew
not to live in fear

walk in love
treat myself with respect
a patient dove
on others I always deflect

the true light
as I stand tall
for the greater, I will fight
even when I fall

Manic Pixie Dream Girl

manic pixie dream girl
she's at it again
watch out for the crash
she needs to be her own friend

up so high on life itself
the music, the colors
like top shelf
nothin' bad in her mind to dwell

adrenaline rush
just another touch
lucid dreaming
another crutch

manic pixie dream girl
she's at it again
watch out for the crash
she needs to be her own friend

when in doubt
she'll pick you up
lift you up
even when she's down

but bow too low
and her brain's on fire
like its gonna blow
gotta go down now

There's So Much More

Letters

I wish I could leave
once and for all
I wish I'd be gone
I wish my time here was done

sick of the interim time
the middle ground
back and forth again
not seeing the how

all over the place
in and out of space
can I please vanish without a trace
because I'm feeling like I don't have a place

I don't feel safe and sound
my feet don't feel firm on the ground
nothing to grab onto, drowning
someone throw me a life saver, quick, I'm panicking

I'm 10-feet under water
my ship is sinking quickly
misery lake
so afraid

I feel so very alone
I feel so disconnected
need a reality check, I'm out of it
need a friend to call home

I've never felt I truly belong
I've always ran and hid
always longed to leave
ever since I was a kid

an attitude of gratitude
they said this could save me
but right now I'm not so thankful
what kind of gift is this present tense life I live?

buck up and white knuckle it through
what if I don't have the strength?
to do this alone
I don't see unity

desiring true calm
desired it all my life
strife has suffocated my mind
honestly I think its broken

can it ever be fixed?
and if this life is just a glimpse
what is the point then?
what's with the front then?

I think the day has come when
enough is enough
I just want to give the fuck up
how can I carry on?

when I truly don't belong
God if you're out there I need a miracle
please bring me some healing
the choices I've made are piling up big

thinking my problems are too much
like I'll never be enough
writing suicide letters to all
so I may cross into nothingness, forever, dissolve

Illusions

confusion in my mind
sometimes chaos is simply an illusion of the sickest kind
fear and pride, gears turning too wide
I tried to be perfect and fight with might
white knucklin' through a facade left me far behind
yet to my delight
a kinder voice appeared so clear
it called me beloved, my sweet dear
now I know we are here for such a reason
this is our season infinitely
no longer do I wonder if anyone else out there got me
may all my life sincerely be
a living reflection of my pure and blissful dreams
visions of clarity
wisdom and unconditional love
this is not fearful or scary
from truth may I never diverge
my God met me right where I was

Head Spins Again

you're here, right now
you're fine, somehow
I'm me, won't back down
sometimes I scream, so loud
life spins around, oh wow
here and gone and there again
my mind spins too
trying to get out, breakdown
corruptions around, NOT NOW!

alone again
my skin frowns
drowning to live
I'm on the prowl
to find a lover, a friend

was I too much?
am I out of luck?
was I not enough?
the worst of hugs
thinking I deserve more than this
manic depression, a full swing and miss
down low, back and forth, gonna blow
wasted away, energy drained today
what else can I say?

alone again
my skin frowns
drowning to live
I'm on the prowl
to find a lover, a friend

There's So Much More

in times of need
I feel defeat
really a moment to stand up
for myself, step in, be my own friend

alone again
my skin frowns
drowning to live
I'm on the prowl
to find a lover, a friend

What I Learned in AA

depression and obsessions
not learning my lesson
stuck in the past
how could I last
living this way?
that I couldn't say

I've been going downhill rapidly
my demons laugh at me
until a stranger caught my eye
as I looked in the mirror, surprised
eyes bloodshot red
scared of my own head

these thoughts in my mind
capture my emotions every time
turmoil strikes deep
trying to get on my own two feet
but I feel so empty
God why did you let me?

turn into this disaster?
yet you've prepared a beautiful pasture
you say, with a gorgeous mansion
how could this happen?
I'm used to living in the trash
where our wills have clashed

self-seeking motivation
I need some elevation
which high do I chase?
one that is of grace?
or one that serves me?
because I so desperately

There's So Much More

need to find peace
staring through the trees
at this beautiful creation
as I feel a strong desperation
to do what is right
and fight this fight

but fear has overcome my mind
afraid that every time I try
it won't be enough
afraid of being unloved
unworthy and alone
so I've stuck to my comfort zone

where there is no growth
as I bulldoze over my hopes
and dreams that I've began to ignore
pushed away so I could find more
of what I think brings me satisfaction
drugs, money, and lust in action

illustrating every move I make
like a puppet on a string, acting fake
I've let these negative things control me
because trauma can be so controlling
wondering what could be my fate
if I stay on this path, how will I be great?

a new revelation
for the duration
of the rest of my life
without living in strife
God said he is loving
and blessings will keep coming

as I noticed he was carrying
me, and my family is not burying
me, because I was protected
and I may have been affected
mentally, but I am still here
so cheerfully, I tell you dear

there is so much hope
when we aren't on dope
passion can be reignited
we just need to choose to fight it
willingness
open-mindedness

I must walk in grace
and not let myself get in the way
the cost of not loving myself is high
truth is, for self-love I was designed
the cost of not loving myself is high
truth is, for self-love I was designed

Time Split

a time split
one minute my heads up in the gutter
then another passes and my heads now under water
thought I knew you all along
now I know that I was wrong

a time split
one minute my words mean something
the next I thought you lost 'em, stomach churning
thought we'd always sing our song
I know now I'm too far gone

a time split
13 years of life ago
a kid, life was all I thought I'd know
playing through the pain
laughter without gain

a time split
fast forward watch me crash
moving past, I think I'll last
loving along my walk of life
ascending to the highest heights

Learning

trusting my gut
my intuition
something I haven't always done
but now it's my mission
not to run
but to take things slow
oh what fun
don't let it blow
bubbling over
another shoulder
I slept on
but did wrong
got tripped up
and out of luck
but I'm believing
someday, somehow
while learning and growing
yet I don't need it all right now

There's So Much More

Am I?

old patterns
are they repeating?
so deceiving
will I be gone completely?

old patterns
anxiety rising
stability dying
yet I keep on trying

stay kind to yourself
even when you doubt
misery lake, not so proud
take my hand, we'll get out

stay kind to yourself
thoughts run our lives
there's nowhere to hide
I've certainly tried

another sunny day
wish I felt the same way
my mind is overcast
cycling through the same old trash

lacking energy today
to battle these waves
scared to repeat the past
am I going to last?

Fake Friends

call me weird, I like the freaks and geeks
friends sometimes are enemies, that can be alright with me
I believe I will make a difference in this world for sure
no stone unturned, as the world keeps turning and I'm no
longer burning

you tell me to try harder, hoping I figure it out
where's the love in your reactions?
hypocrite, I'm not having that any longer
I'll give you space but where is mine at?
you call me weak, and won't let me speak
fearful of your own pride, your own mind
blossoming isn't always what it seems like

call me weird, I like the freaks and geeks
friends sometimes are enemies, that can be alright with me
I believe I will make a difference in this world for sure
no stone unturned, as the world keeps turning and I'm no
longer burning

Fantasy Island

déjà vu; been seeing twos in two
my life; not really sure what to do
I thought I was designed for you
I wish I could just see truth

As Above, So Below

you and me
could we show the world
this human race, more love
every soul, everywhere, deserves to feel
the innovative warmth of the dove
as above

so below
but I feel like a whirlwind
about to hurl
I'm so sorry
I hurt myself too
fear, no tears
I've been this way for years

AFRAID

afraid of the dark
I've been afraid of the dark
a dark basement following, running up the stairs, swallowing
afraid of everything
afraid, afraid, afraid
afraid of everything
even afraid of me

Yin and Yang

this is just a way to vent
a way my time is spent

whether I feel good or bad
when I'm up high or feeling sad

tonight I feel I'm crashing
manic depression fighting
one moment I can have it all
the next I'm not so certain
my brain trying to tell me I'll fall
so I should just close the curtain
the outside world seems so destroyed
and the people I care for, I annoy
lies, lies, lies inside my mind
can I find balance this time?

Control

fear that I will
not get what I need or want
my heart's desires
lead me climbing the ladder faster

fear that I will
be alone and unloved
my intentions
turned to deceptions

fear is so controlling
traumas reinforcing
really lessons that I'm learning
worthy of self-love; deserving

Who Knows? Do I?

in and out of time
what am I gonna do if my words don't rhyme?
what do I get for one more time?
can someone please tell me if I'm outta my mind?
I know I've been designed
to feel and float and fly
but I can't deny
sometimes, yeah sometimes
sometimes when I'm all alone
emotions lie, say I don't belong
like I'll never have a home
might as well hang up the phone
my face should have shown
that I was wrong all along
but that wasn't the tone
why hadn't anyone known?

Rhymes

in and out of time
could I be running out of rhymes?
and who's to say that this time
our worlds won't be jeopardized
wonder why, commit a crime, missing signs
like thoughts I can't deny
until I finally realize
I might be out of my mind
yet I still can't define
or come to terms with the same old lies

I couldn't hide
so I stood to fight

Memory

poetry of memories are melodies surrounding me
astonishing, inspiring, inquiring lessons of my soul
spirit guides, no longer can I hide, the essence where my
divine goals
are intertwined like written rhymes spoken long ago
higher vibrations, frequencies unforsaken, lovely light casting
spells like never before
truly free in simply being me
a love shown in more than glimpses from above
may love grow
self-hatred was truly sinking, diminishing, striking fear and
tears for years below

There's So Much More

Let it Grow

if I love a flower I must let it grow, let it go, slow down and
watch the rivers flow
no time to worry I suppose
my God already knows
even when I don't know
what I'm doing, where I'm going, he assures me, not to worry,
keep on moving, keep on going, never hurry, never stop
glistening, never stepping farther from truth, I hope to keep on
learning and choosing you
you'll never hurt me
this is all for the greater goodness that soothes

Tonight

tonight I feel content
like the things I meant
to do and venting to you
all made sense

tonight I feel up high
we must've reached cloud 9
are you becoming my device
time will tell what we decide

Balance

the sun and the moon
the day and the night
the brightness and darkness
the perpetual marriage

the good news and bad
the happy feelings and the sad
the kindness that guides us
the vibes atmospheric

life must be a gift
in life I must have hope
my life must be priceless
please never give up

To My Man

with you, life's not a race
and I don't want to run away
I love it when you kiss my face
my dear, let us stay and play

keep me in your grace
hold my hand, don't be late
in us, I have tremendous faith
it's all love, no room for hate

I love the way your hair falls into place
I love how you've invited me into your space
there's no rhyme I could say
that describes how I cherish our days

Manic Depression

manic depression
like a full swing and miss
like true love with a diss
moodswings; misery or bliss

manic depression
fighting in my head
indecisive of life itself
would I be better off dead?

maybe life's not so bad
maybe I don't have to be so sad
maybe my time is now to rise and sing
the time is now, can you hear truth ring

perhaps there is a better way
to fight this fight and gladly stay
through peace, letting go, release
not giving up, no retreat

Present

today is the day
I will stand tall
this is the day
I will not fall

the day has come
to stand up for me
Katie, you must not run
fearlessly at peace

There's So Much More

An Unbalance of Sorts

manic depression
an unbalance of sorts
is not the end all
of course

when the funds are low
and the fear is high
you don't have to blow up
or live in disguise

I'm right here with you
although it's hard to see
I need you here with me
remember to breathe

I am never far
you are not abandoned
work hard
it'll happen

manic depression
an unbalance of sorts
is not the end all
of course

I'm feeling a bit all over the place
in and out of space
yet I'm glad to be here
not vanishing without a trace

my footprint of energy I always leave behind
and I hope in every rhyme
there is time of peace
and treating myself so kind

Melodies from the Heart and Soul

hopeful, right from the heart
love is the highest vibration
the only dimension
I want to live in

manic depression is not my label
I won't put myself in a box
I may stay faithful to self
no matter the cost

because my soul is worth more
than torture undeserved
my soul is truly worth more
than torture undeserved

my soul is climbing high
love fills my delight
I'm not afraid of these heights
and I don't need to ask why

manic depression
an unbalance of sorts
is not the end all
of course

just keep going
day by day
just keep going
one foot to the next

keep on yearning
even when the shadows start surfacing
don't give in, blow up
the world is unfolding

There's So Much More

as your highest good is awakening
and trauma is mending
emotions are balancing
keep on meditating

and writing your book
blessed with the perfect way to vent
and connect, these lyrics
mean everything to me

you see
in myself
I finally
believe

manic depression
an unbalance of sorts
is not the end all
of course

My Love

melodies from my fingertips
on this rosewood fretboard
words dancing on my lips
sweet love songs, all yours

All in All

I don't want a piece of you
I want every single part
even when you feel you lose
I'll still play for you my guitar
it's the way you see through
me, when I'm singing in your car
even when I've got the blues
I never want you to move far
I'd even help you tie your shoes
may we never be apart

Translucently

peacefully I am indeed
dreaming, so lucidly
remaining sane
my brain, more tame
resolving traumas translucently

love rains over my face
the dove has landed on its rightful place
truth over fear
visions so clear
letting go of what isn't great

Love Wins

been living on the fear trail
I've walked it up and down
interrupting my thoughts now
gratitude, in love, will not fail

Phoenix

I am truly rising
brokenness doesn't define me
I am whole and loved
fixing my mind state to rise up

There's So Much More

Soar Together

walking down by the river
listening as the current bubbles
thinking I'll just sit here
allow it to take away my troubles

watching two little birds
wondering what they say together
soft melodies from Earth
this is where I find my answer

clues that you and I
could love ourselves a little more
if you've realized
take my hand and we will soar

Grateful to be Thankful

I'm so grateful
that I am here today
I'm so thankful
to grow and to change

I'm so grateful
although I may stumble
I'm so thankful
I desire to be humble

I'm so grateful
I can be my true self
I'm so thankful
I'm taking the right steps

I'm so grateful
I have a job
I'm so thankful
I'm not utterly lost

I'm so grateful
for the hobbies I can practice
I'm so thankful
I don't have to be fractious

I'm so grateful
that I can fight the good fight
I'm so thankful
I'm no longer blinded by night

I'm so grateful
for the connections I'm making
I'm so thankful
they keep me from breaking

There's So Much More

I'm so grateful
for you and for me
I'm so thankful
this is not a dream

I'm so grateful
that I am worthy of love
I'm so thankful
to gain strength from above

I'm so grateful
that in this moment I see clearly
I'm so thankful
my mistakes don't define me

I'm so grateful
I can experience peace
I'm so thankful
that I am free

Acknowledgments

There's So Much More

I would like to thank Dr Daniel Amen, Dr Caroline Leaf, and Dr Nicole LePera (The Holistic Psychologist) for their work and devotion to helping others.

I am very grateful to my counselors and my psychiatrist, Dr P, for truly caring about me and helping me get better.

Fallon Jordan, certified brain health professional, has always been incredibly inspiring and I am grateful for her to have put together the foreword on this book. Her work as a designer and life coach can be found on her website: https://www.fallonjordan.com/

Mac Miller, NF, Ellen Hopkins, and Eminem are my favorite lyricists and the most inspirational artists for my writing style. I applaud Eminem for celebrating 14-years of sobriety in April of 2022.

Russ, who grew up in my hometown, has had tremendous success with his book *It's All in Your Head: Get Out of Your Own Way* and his independent music label *DIEMON (Do It Everyday Music Or Nothing)*.

I would like to acknowledge others who have uplifted my life including Brooke M, Jason W, Kristy F, Tanner G, Marcos S, Tate S, Cynthia H, Meredith H, Taylor W, Bobby J, James H, Terri S, Beka C, Annabelle M, Ariel and Joddy R, Crystal T, Justin S, Victoria E, Kylie B, Liz F, Mary Margaret C, Olivia R, Israel L, Jon N, Sarah T, Nicole P, Kelli C, April S, Lester L, Dustin S, Morgan M, Jeff and Caroline B, Blakeley W, Joe B, David C, Scott B, Jack P, Bill S, Chris M, Matt H, Shane W, Nancy D, Julie P, Tabatha M, Riley M, Timmy L, Madison C, Amy P, Mary R, Brittany N, Callie G, Charlotte M, Debbie R, Eric D, Laura R, Lawrence L, Carla J, Michael H, Bekah D, Lorraine and Tim M, Tammy and Bill M, Joyce Y, Betty C, Jai O, Stefan G, Sam F, Sheyla R, and Todd S.

There's So Much More

Confidential Help

There's So Much More

IN THE US:

-988 Suicide and Crisis Lifeline: 988
24/7, call/ text 988 or chat online at https://988lifeline.org/

-SAMHSA National Helpline: 1-800-662-HELP (4357)
24/7, Substance Abuse and Mental Health Services
Administration

US AND OTHER COUNTRIES:
https://www.helpguide.org/find-help.htm

There's So Much More

About The Author

There's So Much More

Katie Grace was born in Atlanta, Georgia and grew up just north of the big city in Roswell. She is very empathetic, kind, and desires to see the best in others. Katie has a passion for psychology and helping people unleash their own true potential.

Right after her 22nd birthday she was diagnosed with bipolar but didn't fully understand what it meant for her life. A year later, she joined a sober living facility and attended AA meetings. A few months later, Katie came off her medication which threw her into an intense manic episode and was found to be in psychosis. This called for hospitalization.

Katie is now interested in holistic and integrative ways of treatment along with taking daily medications. She understands that her story, including her struggles, is her life's purpose.

There's So Much More

A Note from the Author

There's So Much More

Thank you for reading my story. Although this book was challenging to write, this has been a beautifully healing process. If my poetry inspired you, please leave a review on Amazon.

You can find more of my writing on my website where new content is often posted and there are links to social media, resources, and more.

https://www.blueskysunnyeyes.com/

Made in the USA
Columbia, SC
24 August 2022

66028697R00098